EXPLORING COUNTRIES

Haiti

by Jim Bartell

BELLWETHER MEDIA · MINNEAPOLIS, MN

Note to Librarians, Teachers, and Parents:

Blastoff! Readers are carefully developed by literacy experts and combine standards-based content with developmentally appropriate text.

Level 1 provides the most support through repetition of high-frequency words, light text, predictable sentence patterns, and strong visual support.

Level 2 offers early readers a bit more challenge through varied simple sentences, increased text load, and less repetition of high-frequency words.

Level 3 advances early-fluent readers toward fluency through increased text and concept load, less reliance on visuals, longer sentences, and more literary language.

Level 4 builds reading stamina by providing more text per page, increased use of punctuation, greater variation in sentence patterns, and increasingly challenging vocabulary.

Level 5 encourages children to move from "learning to read" to "reading to learn" by providing even more text, varied writing styles, and less familiar topics.

Whichever book is right for your reader, Blastoff! Readers are the perfect books to build confidence and encourage a love of reading that will last a lifetime!

This edition first published in 2011 by Bellwether Media, Inc.

No part of this publication may be reproduced in whole or in part without written permission of the publisher. For information regarding permission, write to Bellwether Media, Inc., Attention: Permissions Department, 5357 Penn Avenue South, Minneapolis, MN 55419.

Library of Congress Cataloging-in-Publication Data
Bartell, Jim.
 Haiti / by Jim Bartell.
    p. cm. – (Exploring countries) (Blastoff! readers)
 Includes bibliographical references and index.
 Summary: "Developed by literacy experts for students in grades three through seven, this book introduces young readers to the geography and culture of Haiti"–Provided by publisher.
 ISBN 978-1-60014-575-9 (hardcover : alk. paper)
 1. Haiti–Juvenile literature. I. Title.
 F1915.2.B368 2011
 972.94–dc22   2010039125

Contents

Where Is Haiti?

Did you know?

The island of Tortuga lies off the northern coast of Haiti. This island was once a hideout for pirates who sailed throughout the Caribbean!

Cuba

Atlantic Ocean

Tortuga

Windward Passage

Gulf of Gonâve

Haiti

Gonâve Island

★ **Port-au-Prince**

Caribbean Sea

fun fact

Haiti gets its name from the language of the Taino people, the first people to live on Haiti. The Taino word *Ayiti* means "mountainous land."

4

Dominican
Republic

Haiti is a small country in the **Caribbean**. It lies on the western part of Hispaniola, an island it shares with the Dominican Republic. Haiti's mainland and islands cover 10,714 square miles (27,750 square kilometers).

The Windward Passage is a small **strait** that separates Haiti from Cuba. It also links the Atlantic Ocean to the Caribbean Sea. Two **peninsulas** extend from Haiti's mainland into the Caribbean Sea. The **Gulf** of Gonâve sits between the two peninsulas. Its waters surround Gonâve Island, Haiti's largest island. Haiti's capital is Port-au-Prince.

Mountain ranges cover most of Haiti. Many of the ranges extend into the Dominican Republic. The highest mountain is Pic la Selle in southeastern Haiti. It stands 8,793 feet (2,680 meters) tall.

Valleys, **plateaus**, and plains stretch across the rest of Haiti. The Central Plateau sits in the middle of the country. Small plains lie throughout the country, especially along the coasts. The Artibonite River is the largest and longest in Haiti. It begins in the Dominican Republic, flows along the border, and then crosses Haiti to empty into the Gulf of Gonâve.

fun fact

The waters off the coast of Haiti contain many coral reefs. The reefs are home to many plants and animals, including giant sponges!

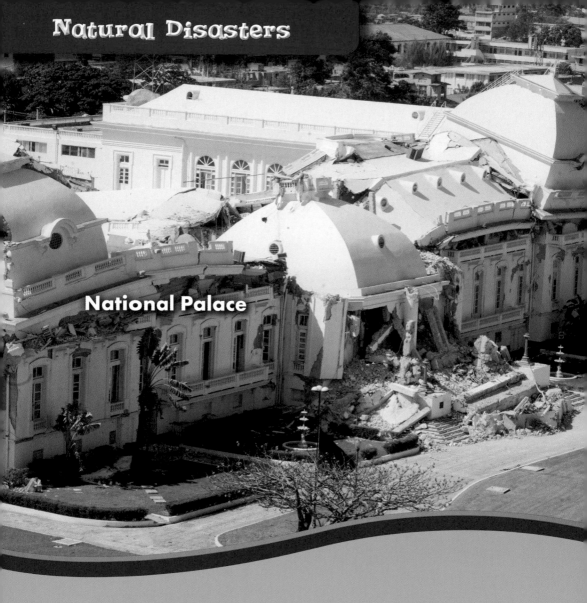

National Palace

Natural disasters often hit Haiti. The country is located on one of Earth's **fault lines**. This causes many earthquakes on the island. On January 12, 2010, a powerful earthquake shook the land near Port-au-Prince. It was followed by more than 50 **aftershocks**. Haiti's National Palace, National **Cathedral**, and many other important buildings crumbled to the ground.

Hurricanes and **tropical storms** also damage Haiti. Years of **deforestation** have left Haiti's land unprotected. With the lack of tree cover, these storms often cause floods and massive **mudslides**. They put Haitians in danger and destroy crops throughout the country.

dugong

Many animals that were **native** to Haiti are now **extinct**. The loss of **habitat** has made it tough for animals to survive. However, frogs, lizards, and snakes can still be found in all parts of Haiti. The country is also home to the black-capped petrel, burrowing owl, and other birds.

solenodon

hutia

caiman

! fun fact

Small crocodiles called caimans live in the rivers of southern Haiti. They share the rivers with American crocodiles, which are much larger!

The hutia and the solenodon are two of only a few remaining native mammals in Haiti. The hutia lives in small forests, while the solenodon lives throughout the country. The solenodon is one of the only mammals in the world that uses its saliva to poison its prey.

Over 9 million people live in Haiti. Most have **ancestors** who were brought from Africa by Europeans. These ancestors worked as slaves on **plantations**. A few Haitians have European and Taino ancestors.

French and Haitian Creole are the two official languages of Haiti. The government, schools, and most businesses use French. Almost all Haitians speak Creole, which is a combination of French, Spanish, African, Arabic, English, and Taino words.

Speak Creole!

English	Creole	How to say it
hello	bonjou	bon-joo
good-bye	orevwa	OR-eh-vwa
yes	wi	wee
no	non	no
please	souple	SOO-play
thank you	mèsi	MES-see
friend	bon zanmi	bon ZAHN-mee

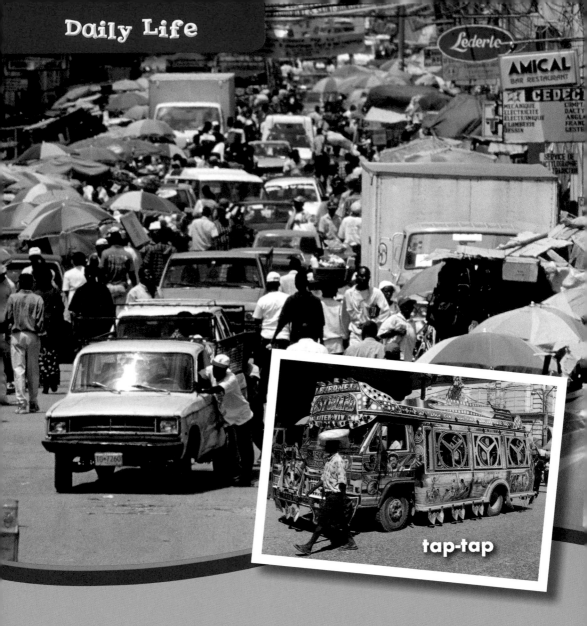

tap-tap

In Haiti's cities, the streets are crowded with people. Haitians buy goods from street markets, food stands, and small shops. Most people live in small shelters built out of any materials they can find. They get from place to place on foot or ride in brightly colored buses called "tap-taps." When riders want to get off the bus, they tap the side and the driver stops.

In the countryside, Haitians live on small plots of land and grow their own food. Most people get around on foot. They build their houses out of scrap wood, mud, and other materials. The few Haitians who can afford houses live on mountainsides. They drive their cars into cities to work.

Where People Live in Haiti

cities
47%

countryside
53%

For most children in Haiti, it is hard to get an education. School is free to attend, but there are few public schools in the country. Many families cannot pay for books, supplies, and uniforms. Children must also speak French because it is the language used in schools. In the city, those who attend school learn math, history, and other subjects. In the countryside, students learn about farming so they can help their parents on the farm. Few students graduate from high school, and an even smaller number go on to study at a university. Haitian families that can afford it often send their children to universities in other countries.

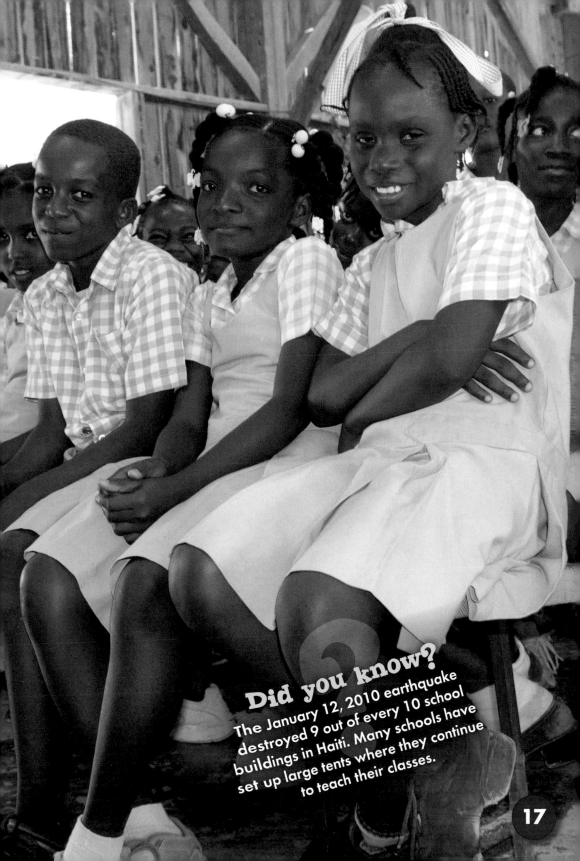

Most Haitians work as farmers. Some grow their own food. Others work on larger farms that grow coffee, sugarcane, mangoes, and other crops. A few farmers raise pigs, cattle, and chickens. Some Haitians work as miners in the countryside. They dig up small amounts of copper, gold, and marble.

In cities, especially Port-au-Prince, many Haitians have **service jobs**. They work in government offices, restaurants, and stores. They often serve visitors from other countries. In factories, workers make cement, clothing, and other products.

Where People Work in Haiti

services 25%

farming 66%

manufacturing 9%

Did you know?

Haitian artists make colorful paintings, sculptures, and quilts. Most works show Haitians and their landscape.

! fun fact

In 1974, Haiti's national soccer team became the first team from the Caribbean to qualify for the World Cup.

Haitians enjoy playing and watching many sports. Soccer is the most popular sport in Haiti. The country has a national team, and most small towns have their own teams. Adults and children also play the sport in empty streets and fields. Haitians who can afford the equipment enjoy tennis and cycling.

Haitians also spend their time playing cards, dominoes, and other games. Many enjoy listening to music and dancing. Storytelling is popular in Haiti. People often gather around storytellers, who use different voices and songs to tell stories.

Did you know?
Many Haitians like to swim. They enjoy the country's rivers, bays, and coastal waters.

Haitian food combines French, African, and Caribbean flavors. Many dishes use peppers and large amounts of **herbs** and spices. Most Haitians eat rice and beans with every meal. These foods are often enjoyed with beef, chicken, or fish. Another common dish throughout the country is *mais moulu*, which is similar to cornmeal. It is often served with *sauce pois*, a sauce made from many kinds of beans. Fried **plantains** are eaten as snacks and during meals. Many kinds of fruits are grown in Haiti. People often drink orange, mango, guava, and other fruit juices.

rice and beans

fried plantains

Independence Day

Haitians celebrate many national and religious holidays. On January 1, they celebrate two holidays. They welcome the New Year and also remember when Haiti declared its independence from France in 1804. The next day, January 2, Haitians celebrate the lives of their ancestors. December 5 is Discovery Day. This marks the day in 1492 when Christopher Columbus discovered Hispaniola.

Most Haitians are Christians. They celebrate Christmas, Easter, and other Christian holidays. Many Haitians also practice **voodoo**, a religion their ancestors brought over from Africa. They worship colorful statues of their gods, or *Loa*. Many voodoo holidays fall on the same days as Christian holidays.

Did you know?

The Citadelle Laferrière had 365 cannons in it to fight the French if they returned. They never did, so stacks of cannonballs still sit in the fort today.

Haiti was once a **colony** of France called Saint-Domingue. The French brought African slaves to the colony to work on coffee and sugarcane plantations. In August of 1791, the slaves rose up in **revolution** against the French landowners. In 1804, the slaves finally won, and the French left the island. This was the first successful slave revolt in history.

In 1807, former slave Henri Christophe became King Henri I of Haiti. He built a large **fort** called Citadelle Laferrière in northern Haiti to defend the country. He also built the Sans-Souci Palace. It was as large as many palaces in Europe. Both of these buildings can still be seen today. They are a reminder to Haitians of their country's proud fight for freedom.

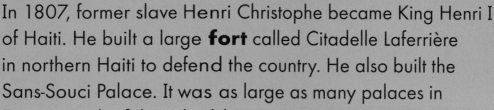

Henri Christophe

Sans-Souci Palace

Fast Facts About Haiti

Haiti's Flag

The flag of Haiti has two horizontal stripes on it. The top stripe is blue and the bottom one is red. The stripes stand for the union between Haitians whose ancestors were from Africa and Haitians whose ancestors come from mixed backgrounds. Haiti's coat of arms is in the middle of the flag, along with text that says, *L'Union Fait la Force*, or "Union Makes Strength." The flag was adopted on February 25, 1986.

Official Name: Republic of Haiti

Area: 10,714 square miles (27,750 square kilometers); Haiti is the 147th largest country in the world.

Capital City:	Port-au-Prince
Important Cities:	Port-de-Paix, Les Cayes, Jacmel, Saint-Marc
Population:	9,648,924 (July 2010)
Official Languages:	French and Haitian Creole
National Holiday:	Independence Day (January 1)
Religions:	Christian (96%), Other (4%); many Haitians also practice voodoo.
Major Industries:	farming, services
Natural Resources:	bauxite, copper, gold, marble
Manufactured Products:	clothing, cement
Farm Products:	coffee, sugarcane, mangoes, rice, corn
Unit of Money:	gourde (French) or goud (Creole); the gourde or goud is divided into 100 centimes (French) or santim (Creole).

Glossary

aftershocks—small earthquakes that follow a larger one in the same area

ancestors—relatives who lived long ago

Caribbean—the area west of the Atlantic Ocean and between North and South America; the Caribbean has many islands, including Haiti.

cathedral—a large church

colony—a territory owned and settled by people from another country

deforestation—the process of cutting down forests

extinct—no longer living

fault lines—cracks in Earth's crust; when the pieces of the crust move, earthquakes occur near fault lines.

fort—a large building made to withstand military attack; forts are often occupied by troops and surrounded by other defenses.

gulf—part of an ocean or sea that extends into land

habitat—the environment in which a plant or animal usually lives

herbs—plants used in cooking; most herbs are used to add flavor to food.

mudslides—large masses of soil that move across the land; mudslides are caused by floods or heavy rain.

native—originally from a specific place

peninsulas—sections of land that extend out from larger pieces of land and are almost completely surrounded by water

plantains—tropical fruits that look like bananas; plantains are often eaten fried in Haiti.

plantations—large farms that grow coffee, cotton, sugarcane, or other crops; plantations are mainly located in warmer climates.

plateaus—areas of flat, raised land

revolution—an uprising of people who change the form of their country's government

service jobs—jobs that perform tasks for people or businesses

strait—a narrow passageway that connects two large bodies of water

tropical storms—powerful storms with strong winds and rain; tropical storms are not as powerful as hurricanes.

voodoo—a religion from Africa; people who practice voodoo worship their ancestors and many gods.

To Learn More

AT THE LIBRARY

Blashfield, Jean F. *Haiti*. New York, N.Y.: Children's Press, 2008.

Callaway, Julie. *My Haiti, My Homeland*. Coconut Creek, Fla.: Educa Vision, 2004.

Temple, Frances. *Taste of Salt: A Story of Modern Haiti*. New York, N.Y.: HarperTrophy, 2005.

ON THE WEB

Learning more about Haiti is as easy as 1, 2, 3.

1. Go to www.factsurfer.com.

2. Enter "Haiti" into the search box.

3. Click the "Surf" button and you will see a list of related Web sites.

With factsurfer.com, finding more information is just a click away.

Index

The images in this book are reproduced through the courtesy of: Ellwood Eppard, front cover, pp. 11 (middle & bottom), 23 (bottom), 29 (top & bottom); Maisei Raman, front cover (flag), p. 28; Jon Eppard, pp. 4-5; Floridastock, pp. 6-7; John A. Anderson, p. 6 (small); Mark Pearson / Alamy, p. 8; MCT via Getty Images, p. 9; Reinhard Dirscherl / Photolibrary, pp. 10-11; Nicholas Smythe / Photo Researchers, Inc., p. 11 (top); Jake Lyell / Alamy, p. 12; Hemis / Alamy, p. 14; Patrick Clinton / Photolibrary, pp. 14 (small), 18 (left & right); Jan A. Csernoch / Alamy, p. 15; Eye Ubiquitous / Photolibrary, pp. 16-17; Mauritius images GmbH / Alamy, p. 19; FIFA via Getty Images, p. 20; JS Callahan/tropicalpix / Alamy, p. 21; Blinkcatcher / Age Fotostock, p. 22; Rohit Seth, p. 23 (top); AFP / Getty Images, p. 24; Alyx Kellington / Photolibrary, p. 25; James P. Blair / Getty Images, p. 26; DEA / G DAGLI ORTI / Photolibrary, p. 27; Getty Images, p. 27 (small).